CW01210371

QUARANTINE:
:CONTAGION

QUARANTINE:
:CONTAGION
Brian Henry

2009

Published by Arc Publications,
Nanholme Mill, Shaw Wood Road
Todmorden OL14 6DA, UK
www.arcpublications.co.uk

Copyright © Brian Henry, 2009

Design by Tony Ward
Printed in Great Britain by the MPG Books Group,
Bodmin and King's Lynn

978 1904614 73 9
978 1906570 13 2

ACKNOWLEDGEMENTS

Originally published in 2006 under the title *Quarantine* by
Ahsahta Press, Boise State University, Idaho, USA.

Some of the poems in this book were first published in the following magazines: *The Antioch Review, Colorado Review, Conjunctions, Fence, The Kenyon Review, Maisonneuve* (Canada), *Notre Dame Review, Prairie Schooner, Third Coast* and *Virginia Quarterly Review.*

The author wishes to thank the Poetry Society of America for awarding *Quarantine* the 2003 Alice Fay Di Castagnola Award, and also Andrew Zawacki and Timothy Liu for their invaluable advice on the manuscript.

Cover photograph by Phoebe Ward © 2009

This book is in copyright. Subject to statutory exception and to provision of relevant collective licensing agreements, no reproduction of any part of this book may take place without the written permission of Arc Publications.

Arc International Poets Editor: John Kinsella

for Tomaž

CONTENTS

Quarantine / 11
Contagion / 63

Biographical Note / 79

QUARANTINE:

QUARANTINE

By the time the sun touched the grass
beneath my back where I lay
beside my wife and son who seemed
to be breathing a fog of breath
I thought hung above each mouth
I knew I had died and was dead
though thinking through where I was
as if the thinking could bring me
where death is not an is
instead of where I found myself
watching my wife and son without
seeing them beside me on the ground
but knowing they were there
breathing as I was the air above
the mouths there and perhaps thinking
as I was thinking to keep myself here
where I could not be dead could not be
dead could not be anything but alive
and tracking the sun coming over the trees
even though the moon had not moved
and my wife my son and I were growing
into the grass beneath us and the moon
does not care about the bodies there
in that field on the earth at dawn
the moon cannot see and if
the moon could see it still would not care

QUARANTINE / 2

An attempt at truth when truth
is what is most difficult to hold down
the three bodies in the grass
stable there as they we lose composition
and become an else a handful of elses
in a field beneath the moon as it is replaced
by the sun now risen above the trees
and starving the grass of dew
the sun showing three bodies there
a dog stepping from the trees

QUARANTINE / 3

A dog from the trees
a familiar image if not for the angle
the dog now at my feet I see it
from where I lie wonder if it will bite
from fear from hunger anger
hunger having nothing to do with emotion
though it too is a feeling
and wonder if I will be eaten
dead and dead will I feel the teeth
take pieces of me what was me
away pieces of my wife and son
and what will remain will anything
remain for the moon not to see
when it reveals its blue scrapes
to those watching it from here
but when the dog touches its mouth
to me it tugs at a boot pulls it off
and steps into the trees at the other side

QUARANTINE / 4

We had been pulled from the trees
at the other side by the feet
by men in charge of clearing
the town of the sick the dying
the dead dead we were cleared
I remember my son died first
my wife three days after
I was relieved to hear him stop
screaming whenever he screamed
I felt like screaming my wife
only cried she blamed me for
she blamed me for everything
I had brought it into our house
I was the cause for his death for hers
she never mentioned mine
though I was as close to death as she

QUARANTINE / 5

As close to death as she I asked her
how she felt if she was happy now
at last knowing she had been right
if being right brought joy if
it was in itself a virtue
if rightness could be a source of joy
without knowing one were right
I know I was smiling as I spoke
as I myself was dying and she said nothing
I could hear she said something
but I could not hear the words
and I screamed I screamed as my son
had screamed not at her but for my son
and then of course she died
not in her sleep but with her eyes open

QUARANTINE / 6

My wife died with her eyes open
but her eyes were not on me
when she died I was not there
when she died

QUARANTINE / 7

When she died I was at the river
though forbidden to leave for any reason
my throat a fleshy burn I left
the house to find water
knew the river too was dying
but the dying are not afraid
of being killed so I left
and told my wife I hoped she died
happy at least knowing she knew
I hoped she died in pain hoping
she knew I hoped she died in pain
and after drinking the water I returned
to her open dead face our son
still in her arms even then
the white scarf still in one hand
I knew I would not drink again
the water more painful than its absence
a jagged fire in the mouth and a knot
in the stomach as nothing came out

QUARANTINE / 8

There is a bell to ring when
a body succumbs I rang this bell
for my son but no one came
I did not ring it for my wife
and no one came no one here
is alive to take the bodies
no one wants to take the bodies
away if I were not dead
I would not touch me alive
or dead I would not touch me

QUARANTINE / 9

I feel nothing lying here I feel little
here the sores on my legs
on my neck have not been drained
the pain almost glorious so familiar
in its presence during the night
but now there is a softness
to the feeling a body is washing
away falling into the grass beneath it
and that body was mine and no one
is here to carry it no one will hold the body

The dog has found a tree beside which to chew the boot it took from the dead man in the field. A dog will not approach a dead woman but will sit or lie beside a dead man until someone comes for the dog/to remove the body. A dog cannot see a dead child but knows something dead is there. A dog can learn to adapt to new scenarios. Few dogs have found a dead woman with a dead man. The dog cannot ignore the body of the dead man, wants to ignore the body of the dead woman, does not see the body of the dead boy, so the dog takes something from the man, does not approach the woman, does not see the boy. The field is fresh with death, the dog knows. Having found a dead man and woman together, the dog will not retrace its steps. The dog feels something like happiness having part of the man here with it in the woods. It chews the boot and forgets about the dead man and woman until some days later when it steps from the trees into the field. It knows the death there is no longer fresh, knows the bodies there are no longer there, and turns from the field to walk back into the woods.

QUARANTINE / 10

I feel sad about many things my life
being the main thing
it lacks texture lacks matter
its arc like every other arc
I wish I had never had a son
sons always hate their fathers
I had no wish for a daughter
no wife no lover no no

QUARANTINE / 11

I wish I had not fainted
when at fifteen I had tried to remove
the knife so sharp and I awoke alone
on the floor the knife on the floor
and without a mirror I could not know
and slept until my mother woke me

QUARANTINE / 12

When my mother woke me she asked
about the bloody rag the knife the blood
on the floor she asked why my face
was swollen so I knew I had failed
but no longer cared and did not care enough
to answer her not even when she cried
and though tempted to cry with her
I left for the river and let a man there
touch me inside he ripped something
inside and he told me my scars
would be beautiful when they healed
and I knew he was wrong but chose to
believe him as he held me against him
even in his sleep he held me against him

QUARANTINE / 13

In his sleep he held me and I wanted
the smell of him to stay on me
wanted my mother to smell him on me
and tell my father so he could kill me
and I know they thought I loved him
though I loved only his smell after
he was through with me I loved
nothing wanted nothing or no one
and my mother one morning
my father could not speak to me
told me I would be married that year
or my father would kill her
not me or the man at the river but her
and I was married that year

QUARANTINE / 14

I was married that year
but still went to the river
even after he stopped meeting me
there some nights I watched the water
alone some nights I wished her
my wife not my mother
dead and some nights a man
or a boy would find me
or a group of boys and hurt me
but I knew they wanted to love me
the hate in their muscles a false hate
one night I was thrown into the river
one night held down by two boys
as another tried to finish me
and still I went to the river

QUARANTINE / 15

I went to the river most nights
and returned home near dawn
to sleep briefly before work
and I slept again briefly before dusk
and my wife knew where I went
and she knew why but said nothing
could smell the men on me
the water and dirt their semen and sweat
and she hated me from our beginning
and until she died she hated
I wonder if she hates me now in death
her love so far from where I was
I cannot remember how our son was born
cannot remember when or how

QUARANTINE / 16

I suppose the boy has another father
still alive perhaps and waiting for me
to die before reclaiming what was his
I cannot remember lying down
with the boy's mother not once
but there is a lot I cannot remember
and I frequently walked through days
asleep I slept as I worked asleep
is the way I was wanted by the world
was a way of being in the world

The moon seemed to glow as it hovered above the river. Brighter than the stars around it, it was reflected in most of the water below it. The river, too filthy to reflect, could not catch the moon. The young man sitting by the tree did not look at the moon; he seemed to be searching the river for it. Three other young men, one bouncing as he walked, approached him from his right. Only when they stopped between him and the river did he look up. He motioned for them to sit beside him. The four sat there watching the river until the sun broke behind them.

QUARANTINE / 17

I never played with the boy
never touched him except to pinch
as if to see if he was truly there
or was my wife's own invention
I never fed or bathed him never spoke
to him except by mistake his mother
did all those things and seemed
to do them well though he screamed
as much as I had heard anyone to
my own words when he heard them
were intended not for him but for me
and when I tried to break them back
out of him his mother would step between
he looked like no one I knew

QUARANTINE / 18

I found many things at the river
things discarded and lost stolen
and lost everything ends up in water
the river the earth's least committed owner
it gives up most of what it finds
to people searching it or to what it feeds into
but I cannot remember anything I found
since I gave everything I found
to the boys I met at the river
I either gave the things or had them taken
some nights I used the things to convince
a boy to touch me to be touched
entered in as many ways as I could think
to enter a body spread next to me
his body an offering my sacrifice

The young man sitting by the river grabbed a stick, swung it at the boy with the sack beside him. The boy spun to one side and ran. The young man ran after him. Leeches fell from the sack. Trembled when they hit the ground.

QUARANTINE / 19

I met a woman who read the future
in the faces of those who had futures
I told her I had no future
that I was living in a feature
less present threatening to extend forever
that I would give up my face
I thought she would scoff
attribute what I said to fever
but she saw the scars around my face
and instead of pressing she left
left me with my river my craft
my constant present still without features

QUARANTINE / 20

My craft was to know what would appear
in the river each night as it was carried
what could arrive lost or discarded
lost in the river until I found it
I took some of the things and sold them
took some as gifts for the boys
but more often watched them pass

QUARANTINE / 21

My wife tried to kill me once in bed
a knife at my throat she told me
to say something to speak to her
or she would cut out my tongue
I said please and she stabbed me
in the neck I lay in bed waiting to die
but I only fell asleep I did not dream
awoke with the knife next to me
and her standing by the door watching
perhaps now you will speak to me
I sat up grabbed the knife and held it
toward her she opened the door to flee
I licked the blood off the blade
and fell asleep again this time with dreams

The young man approaches the river as if asleep, walks with his eyes on the ground. He is so thin the river would spin him away without effort. He sits by a tree overlooking the water. He watches the water. A boy approaches the river from the other side with a sharp stick in his hand. He slides down the bank and wades to his knees and waits, occasionally thrusts the spear into the water. He does not change his position in the river. After an hour he pulls the spear out of the water, a fish flapping on its point. The boy jumps out of the river, using the spear's blunt end for leverage as he climbs the bank. When he reaches the top he runs.

QUARANTINE / 22

I picked up my son as he cried
he was constantly crying
his mother cooking saw
and screamed and the boy screamed
so I shook him tried to twist him
in half he would not break
I threw him against the wall
and smiled to hear something snap
his spine I hoped his back
his mother rushed him into her arms
and I saw the crack in the wall
the wall cracked at the impact
the boy though upset was not broken
his mother ran with him out the door
as I grabbed the chair I had been sitting in
and stepped toward the wall

QUARANTINE / 23

I never liked stories they always ended
and endings are too much like beginnings
in their rejection of silence
silence for me was never a choice
but a necessity arising from habit
and no one seemed to honour silence
always talking singing telling stories
as if death as if pain as if joy
could be postponed avoided found
by the words buttressed against the quiet
my son screamed until his death he screamed
into death my wife said nothing
she did not scream like my son
she died just the same hot and in pain
I will die silent I will tell my story as I die

QUARANTINE / 24

In the field I was not dead
though soon
my wife and son
my wife and notmyson
beside me were dead
I speak here so

The young man paces the room with an infant in his arms. Crying, he wipes the baby's forehead with a rag. He circles for some time, several hours, until the woman stands up from the chair she had collapsed into earlier and holds out her arms. The young man eases the baby into her arms. His arms now empty, he sobs so hard he almost loses consciousness.

QUARANTINE / 25

Once a boy fished for an evening
in front of me at the river
he had come from the other side
of the river I had never crossed
I never wanted to cross the river
but when he caught a fish
he brought it to me instead of returning
from where he came he offered
the fish to me and I took his hand instead
he slept with me until the sun
woke us both where we lay

QUARANTINE / 26

The boy was not beautiful but he was mine
that evening and until dawn
I touched him as he slept
I turned him onto his stomach
and eased his clothing off
the fish had been eaten raw
the boy had insisted I eat its entrails
for strength my fingers slick
with its oils and innards my mouth
alive with the fish I lay
on his back and moved a pulse
of flesh hard against his back
I became the spill on his back
I did not enter him that night

QUARANTINE / 27

I entered him at dawn I
entered him as he left at dawn
as he had entered the river as the fish
had left the river and entered our bodies
our bodies so different from the water
I wanted him to give birth to a son
to swell and call it my love his flesh
so tight he would burst from the weight
a weight inside him a child a stone
he was not beautiful too burnt and too thin
he was all angle and no curve

Just before dawn, the young man's wife woke and turned toward him. She saw a cream-coloured blister on his neck. He slept as the blister turned red and then black in her mind. He slept, she wept. The baby woke, the young man slept.

QUARANTINE / 28

My father woke before dawn to work
and returned after dusk his work
is what he was a long series of days
inside his body which did not change
as he aged always ugly and hard
the hair on his legs worn away
by the heavy pants he was forced
by his work to wear the hair on the backs
of his hands singed by the work his face dark
I heard about it at the river a man spoke
of bodies turned out from the inside
there were graves everywhere
not enough lime for them all everywhere
clothing and bedding being burned

QUARANTINE / 29

I knew I would die before my mother
would kill my wife and father
I never wanted a son or daughter
I have none never heard laughter
until the bodies were loaded into water
two men pulled carts piled with corpses
the death was giving work even to lepers
the men stopped near the bank and flipped
each body onto the ground dragged it
by the feet to where the ground dropped
toward the river and pushed they laughed
as they worked laughed when one stopped
to vomit into the river as the bodies fell
into the water where a boy stood with a torch
to set them on fire he had no sense of touch
his hands were charred from what he held

QUARANTINE / 30

Wine when I drank it would send me
to sleep I rarely drank unlike my father
he drank as long as I can remember
his face puckered from it all redder
as he aged his face a bulbous mass
I kicked him once by accident in the face
a man and his son playing his big jaw
smacked he swung so hard at my head
I could taste the blood before his hand

QUARANTINE / 31

Fire brought to the water by flesh
for days the river burned
birds rode the bodies flapping
themselves into the air to avoid flames
a vulture forgot itself in its feeding
a tip of a wing caught the bird
lifted and dove to put out the fire
and did not emerge the river
never blue before was now blue
moving pockets of blue

Returning from work shortly before dark, the young man walks through the village rather than around. Beside a street near the village's south edge, four men are digging a giant hole. Their faces are masked, their hands gloved. On one side of the hole there are six carts, at least three bodies to a cart. The men dig with their backs to the bodies.

QUARANTINE / 32

My father drowned in his bath
the year after I married a fitting death
for one so wedded to the earth
he hated water he rarely bathed
if one could die from stench
some nights at the river I thought
myself into his body slipped beneath
the water as he did lost my breath
as he did and forced myself not to fight
the lack of air as it bloomed inside me
as it did in him I like to think I held him
down when he struggled up for air
but I know he died asleep asleep
before his head went under he died
without pain in his stupor he died

Near midday, the young man working, a beaked figure in a mask knocks at his door. The beaked figure wears a leather hat, leather boots, leather gloves. He sets the stick he has been carrying beside the door, does not remove his hat as he enters. He takes the baby from its mother, moves his free hand across its abdomen, arms, legs, and neck. He does not remove his gloves, the beak, or the mask. Returns the baby to its mother, pulls three leeches from a sack. Lances and drains the bubo at its groin. Applies an ointment of Theriac.

QUARANTINE / 33

Whom to address when there is no one
I wonder lying here with one boot on
my wife never listened my son
too young to hear the dog has gone
back to the trees to gnaw its song
started at dusk and quickly stopped
strange how I feel my foot the cold
the sky today was so clear it hurt
tonight the clouds will bring their wet
to rain within the confines of violence
so wordless the trees sway to drip
their leaves onto the fallen
I am the only one here who is falling

QUARANTINE / 34

I am the only one here who is falling
everyone else should be forgotten
my mother my father the wife her son
they were only props in
figures against which to measure a life
I lived as much as I could
at night I lived I moved in the dark
I think I explained that once
how I went to the river wanting
how I left my soul there burning

QUARANTINE / 35

Though I rarely slept I never missed sleep
I had learned to move as little as necessary
to work without effort to watch my wife
and son cry from hunger he cried in his sleep
my wife never spoke to me except to say
she would kill me but she never raised a hand
she did not leave I wanted her to leave but
I never needed more sleep until I saw
the bodies on fire in the river for days I saw
them blue and orange against a black sky
they would be black in the day without colour
and the birds and the ants would settle on
settle into them until they were only ash
the river having kept them from burning
I was not sad at seeing them I knew I would
be a body burning blue in the river orange
to black this is not why I could not sleep
and only when the bodies stopped did it stop
the strain of such alertness then I slept

QUARANTINE / 36

I sought the dark in order
to dazzle my life a horizon
line on the plains I cleared
my life of closeness nor did
the trees or stones remain
any longer in their places

The young man removes the leeches from his wife's body, wraps her in the quilt from their bed. He stoops to pick up the body, carries it toward the door. Stops to vomit, drags her body the rest of the way. The baby, wrapped the day before, lies beside the bed. All salt, the young man cannot cry.

QUARANTINE / 37

I was so much at the river I do not know
when the death entered me or how
the smoke from the bodies fell on me
men fell on me boys fell was wet
some nights with the smell the smoke
was after I did not go into the river after
the bodies saw no one after the bodies
no one touched me or tried to break
no one touched me at the river

The young man waits outside for a man with a cart. His wife and his son will be taken, piled into a pit near the river, and covered with lime. When at dusk no man has come, the young man unwraps his wife's body, places their son on her chest, and wraps the quilt around both bodies. He carries them away from the river until he is too weak to carry them. He drags them until he is too weak to drag them. The moon nearly full above him, he drops them, collapses beside what he has dropped.

QUARANTINE / 38

No one touched me at the river
but still I am falling I have fallen
into so much and still I am falling

QUARANTINE / 39

So much attention
required by dying
I wish I had been
the first among us
then I would not be
charged with tying
everything together
I am not the only
person with a memory
who wants to be spared
a memory this story

QUARANTINE / 40

If I could burrow into the dirt
beneath my back I would fracture
the earth to return and forget
the river and the nights I already have
forgotten what I have done portioned
into parcels memories I have lost
and now that I cannot see my thoughts
and movements are based on smell
the scent of death is black the sores
are black my wife's skin my son's
dry in the air now that there is no sweat
to keep their bodies which shivered in their heat
cold when I touched them dragged them
by the feet into this field they were cold
like my own hands and face are
they are dead and though I call myself dead
I have not died the words still move across
my face everything right now in the telling

:CONTAGION

Contagion

My face everything right now in the telling.
I have not died the words still move across.
They are dead and though I call myself dead.
To keep their bodies which shivered in their heat.
Are black my wife's skin my son's.
And now that I cannot see my thoughts.
The river and the nights I already have.

Contagion / 2

Who wants to be spared.
I am not the only.
Charged with tying.
The first among us.

Contagion / 3

Into so much and still I am falling.
No one touched me at the river.

Contagion / 4

No one touched me or tried to break.
The bodies saw no one after the bodies.
Some nights with the smell the smoke.
The smoke from the bodies fell on me.
I was so much at the river I do not know.

Contagion / 5

The trees or stones remain.
To dazzle my life a horizon.

Contagion / 6

The strain of such alertness then I slept.
And only when the bodies stopped did it stop.
The river having kept them from burning.
They would be black in the day without colour.
The bodies on fire in the river for days I saw.
I never needed more sleep until I saw.
My wife never spoke to me except to say.

Contagion / 7

How I left my soul there burning.
How I went to the river wanting.
At night I lived I moved in the dark.
Figures against which to measure a life.
My mother my father the wife her son.
I am the only one here who is falling.

Contagion / 8

I am the only one here who is falling.
So wordless the trees sway to drip.
Tonight the clouds will bring their wet.
The sky today was so clear it hurt.
Strange how I feel my foot the cold.
Started at dusk and quickly stopped.
Back to the trees to gnaw its song.
Too young to hear the dog has gone.
My wife never listened my son.
Whom to address when there is no one.

Contagion / 9

But I know he died asleep asleep.
Down when he struggled up for air.
The lack of air as it bloomed inside me.
As he did and forced myself not to fight.
Myself into his body slipped beneath.
For one so wedded to the earth.

Contagion / 10

Moving pockets of blue.
Never blue before was now blue.
Lifted and dove to put out the fire.
For days the river burned.

Contagion / 11

I could taste the blood before his hand.

Contagion / 12

His hands were charred from what he held.
Into the water where a boy stood with a torch.
To vomit into the river as the bodies fell.
The death was giving work even to lepers.
Two men pulled carts piled with corpses.
Until the bodies were loaded into water.
I never wanted a son or daughter.
Would kill my wife and father.
I knew I would die before my mother.

Contagion / 13

Not enough lime for them all everywhere.
Of bodies turned out from the inside.
Of his hands singed by the work his face dark.
The hair on his legs worn away.
Is what he was a long series of days.
My father woke before dawn to work.

Contagion / 14

He was all angle and no curve.
He was not beautiful too burnt and too thin.
A weight inside him a child a stone.
So tight he would burst from the weight.
I entered him at dawn I.

Contagion / 15

I became the spill on his back.
Of flesh hard against his back.
Alive with the fish I lay.
The boy had insisted I eat its entrails.
And eased his clothing off.
I turned him onto his stomach.
The boy was not beautiful but he was mine.

Contagion / 16

He slept with me until the sun.
I never wanted to cross the river.
He had come from the other side.

Contagion / 17

I speak here so.
Beside me were dead.
In the field I was not dead.

Contagion / 18

I will die silent I will tell my story as I die.
Into death my wife said nothing.
By the words buttressed against the quiet.
As if death as if pain as if joy.
And no one seemed to honour silence.

Contagion / 19

And stepped toward the wall.
The boy though upset was not broken.
The wall cracked at the impact.
And I saw the crack in the wall.
His mother rushed him into her arms.
I threw him against the wall.
And screamed and the boy screamed.
I picked up my son as he cried.

Contagion / 20

And fell asleep again this time with dreams.
Perhaps now you will speak to me.

Contagion / 21

But more often watched them pass.
What could arrive lost or discarded.
In the river each night as it was carried.
My craft was to know what would appear.

Contagion / 22

Attribute what I said to fever.
That I would give up my face.
I told her I had no future.
In the faces of those who had futures.

Contagion / 23

To enter a body spread next to me.
A boy to touch me to be touched.
And lost everything ends up in water.
I found many things at the river.

Contagion / 24

He looked like no one I knew.
Out of him his mother would step between.
And when I tried to break them back.
My own words when he heard them.
As much as I had heard anyone to.

Contagion / 25

Was a way of being in the world.
Is the way I was wanted by the world.
Asleep I slept as I worked asleep.
But there is a lot I cannot remember.
I cannot remember lying down.

Contagion / 26

Cannot remember when or how.
Her love so far from where I was.
I wonder if she hates me now in death.
The water and dirt their semen and sweat.
And she knew why but said nothing.
And my wife knew where I went.

Contagion / 27

And still I went to the river.
As another tried to finish me.
Or a group of boys and hurt me.
My wife not my mother.
Alone some nights I wished her.
There some nights I watched the water.
Even after he stopped meeting me.

Contagion / 28

Or my father would kill her.
Told me I would be married that year.
Nothing wanted nothing or no one.
And I know they thought I loved him.
Wanted my mother to smell him on me.
The smell of him to stay on me.

Contagion / 29

Even in his sleep he held me against him.
Inside and he told me my scars.
I left for the river and let a man there.
On the floor she asked why my face.

Contagion / 30

And without a mirror I could not know.
On the floor the knife on the floor.

Contagion / 31

No wife no lover no.
I had no wish for a daughter.
Its arc like every other arc.

Contagion / 32

Is here to carry it no one will hold the body.
And that body was mine and no one.

Contagion / 33

Or dead I would not touch me.
Away if I were not dead.
And no one came no one here.
For my son but no one came.

Contagion / 34

A jagged fire in the mouth and a knot.
The white scarf still in one hand.

Contagion / 35

When she died I was not there.
But her eyes were not on me.

Contagion / 36

Not in sleep but with her eyes open.
And then of course she died.
As I myself was dying and she said nothing.
As close to death as she I asked her.

Contagion / 37

I was the cause for his death for hers.
She blamed me for everything.
Screaming whenever he screamed.
I remember my son died first.
We had been pulled from the trees.

Contagion / 38

But when the dog touches its mouth.
Remain for the moon not to see.
Away pieces of my wife and son.
Take pieces of me what was me.
Dead and dead will I feel the teeth.

Contagion / 39

A dog stepping from the trees.
And starving the grass of dew.
In a field beneath the moon as it is replaced.
And become an else a handful of elses.
The three bodies in the grass.

Contagion / 40

In that field on the earth at dawn.
Does not care about the bodies there.
And my wife my son and I were growing.
Even though the moon had not moved.
And tracking the sun coming over the trees.
Where I could not be dead could not be.
Breathing as I was the air above.
Watching my wife and son without.
Instead of where I found myself.
Where death is not an is.
As if the thinking could bring me.
Beside my wife and son who seemed.
Beneath my back where I lay.
By the time the sun touched the grass.

BIOGRAPHICAL NOTE

BRIAN HENRY was born in Columbus, Ohio in 1972, and raised in Virginia. He has published more than 400 poems in magazines around the world, including *The New Republic, American Poetry Review, The Paris Review, Grand Street, Poetry Review,* and *Jacket*. His poetry has been collected in many anthologies and has been translated into Russian, Slovenian, and Croatian. He was a Fulbright Scholar in Australia in 1997-98 and poetry editor of *Meanjin* that year.

In 2000, Arc Publications published his first book of poetry, *Astronaut*, which was subsequently shortlisted for the Forward Prize. *Astronaut* also appeared in Slovenia in translation from Mondena Publishing in 2000, and in the United States in 2002 from Carnegie Mellon University Press. Salt Publishing released his second book, *American Incident*, in 2002. His third book, *Graft*, appeared in 2003 from New Issues Press in the United States and from Arc in England. His fourth book, *Quarantine*, appeared from Ahsahta Press in 2006; *Quarantine* won the 2003 Alice Fay di Castagnola Award from the Poetry Society of America and was nominated for the Pulitzer Prize and the National Book Award. His fifth book, *The Stripping Point*, was published by Counterpath Press in 2007. A limited edition book, *In the Unlikely Event of a Water*, appeared from Equipage in England in 2007.

Henry has reviewed poetry for the *New York Times Book Review*, the *Times Literary Supplement, The Kenyon Review, Boston Review, The Yale Review,* and *Poetry Review*, among other publications, and his criticism has appeared in *The Antioch Review, The Georgia Review, Virginia Quarterly Review, The Iowa Review,* and other magazines. Henry has co-edited *Verse* since 1995, and he co-edited *The Verse Book of Interviews* (2005).

His translation of the Slovenian poet Tomaž Šalamun's *Woods and Chalices* appeared from Harcourt in 2008, and his translation of Aleš Šteger's *The Book of Things* is forthcoming from BOA Editions.

Also available in the
ARC PUBLICATIONS
International Poets series

LOUIS ARMAND (Australia)
Inexorable Weather

DAVID BAKER (USA)
Treatise on Touch

DON COLES (Canada)
Someone has Stayed in Stockholm

ALISON CROGGON (Australia)
The Common Flesh

KEKI DARUWALLA (India)
The Glass-Blower

SARAH DAY (Australia)
New & Selected Poems

GAIL DENDY (South Africa)
Painting the Bamboo Tree

ROBERT GRAY (Australia)
Lineations

MICHAEL S. HARPER (USA)
Selected Poems

SASKIA HAMILTON (USA)
Canal

ALAMGIR HASHMI (Pakistan)
The Ramazan Libation

DENNIS HASKELL (Australia)
Samuel Johnson in Marrickville

DINAH HAWKEN (New Zealand)
Small Stories of Devotion

BRIAN HENRY (USA)
Graft
Astronaut

RICHARD HOWARD (USA)
Trappings

T. R. HUMMER (USA)
Bluegrass Wasteland

ANDREW JOHNSTON (New Zealand)
Sol
The Open Window

JOHN KINSELLA (Australia)
Comus – A Mask
America (A Poem)
Lightning Tree
The Silo:
A PASTORAL SYMPHONY
The Undertow:
NEW & SELECTED POEMS
Landbridge:
AN ANTHOLOGY OF CONTEMPORARY AUSTRALIAN POETRY
ED. JOHN KINSELLA

ANTHONY LAWRENCE (Australia)
Strategies for Confronting Fear

THOMAS LUX (USA)
The Street of Clocks

J.D. McCLATCHY (USA)
Division of Spoils

TRACY RYAN (Australia)
Hothouse

MARY JO SALTER (USA)
A Kiss in Space

ANDREW SANT (Australia)
The Unmapped Page

ELIZABETH SMITHER (New Zealand)
A Question of Gravity

C.K. STEAD (New Zealand)
Dog
The Right Thing
Straw into Gold

ANDREW TAYLOR (Australia)
The Stone Threshold

JOHN TRANTER (Australia)
The Floor of Heaven